D1532890

FEB 0 1 2011

KANSAS CITY PUBLIC LIBRARY

# SNOUTS, SPINES, & SCUTES

Lynn M. Stone

Rourke
Publishing LLC
Vero Beach, Florida 32964

© 2009 Rourke Publishing LLC

All rights reserved. No part of this book may be reproduced or utilized in any form or by any means, electronic or mechanical including photocopying, recording, or by any information storage and retrieval system without permission in writing from the publisher.

www.rourkepublishing.com

PHOTO CREDITS: © Lynn Stone: title page, page 4, 5, 7, 8, 9, 11, 13, 14, 15, 17, 18, 19, 20, 21; © Matt Matthews: page 6; © Elianet Ortiz: page 10; © Dennis Sabo: page 12; © Robert Blanchard: page 16

Editor: Meg Greve

Cover design by: Nicola Stratford, bdpublishing.com

Interior design by: Renee Brady

**Library of Congress Cataloging-in-Publication Data**

Stone, Lynn M.

Snouts, spines, and scutes / Lynn M. Stone.
    p. cm. --  (What animals wear)
  Includes index.
  ISBN: 978-1-60472-311-3 (hardcover)
  ISBN: 978-1-60472-789-0 (softcover)
  1.  Nose--Juvenile literature. 2.  Spines (Zoology)--Juvenile literature. 3.
Scales (Reptiles)--Juvenile literature.  I. Title.
  QL947S66 2009
  591.47'7--dc22
                            2008012973


Printed in the USA

CG/CG

# Table of Contents

Snouts 4

Spines 12

Scutes 18

Glossary 22

Index 24

# Snouts

Animal **snouts** may be cute or funny looking to us. To an animal, a snout is just useful. It is an animal's nose, and it helps an animal survive.

A pig's upturned snout helps it plow into dirt to find food, like roots.

5

The elephant's snout is amazing. It grasps food and sucks up water.

The elephant's trunk, or snout, is very sensitive to touch and smell.

The **elephant seal** has a curled, baggy snout. A male elephant seal blows air through the snout to make a trumpeting noise.

A big male elephant seal, which can weigh up to 8,000 pounds (3,636 kilograms), bellows to scare other male elephant seals away from his females.

9

Many ocean **predators** have streamlined snouts. With their slim snouts, sharks and dolphins swim easily through the sea to hunt prey.

The bottlenose dolphin uses its toothy snout to catch fish.

# Spines

Some animals have **spines** for protection. Many different kinds of insects, fish, reptiles, and **mammals** have spines.

The sea urchin's spines make it the pincushion of the sea. Some kinds of sea urchins have poisonous spines.

The porcupine looks like a pincushion on land. Some people think a porcupine can throw its spines, but it cannot.

*Porcupine spines easily pull away from the porcupine when they stick into another animal.*

15

Some birds in the chicken and turkey family have a foot spine called a spur. Males fight with their spurs.

A rooster uses its sharp spur as a weapon to fight other roosters.

17

# Scutes

Some kinds of turtles have large scales called **scutes** on their shells. Snakes have scutes on their bellies.

Scutes

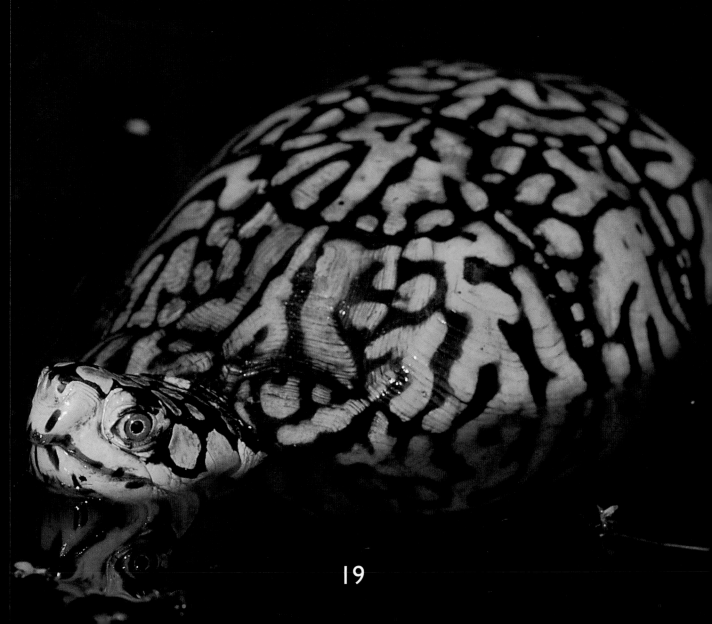

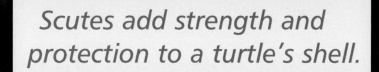
*Scutes add strength and protection to a turtle's shell.*

Snouts, spines, and scutes help animals stay alive. Each kind of animal has its own special features.

The rhino, with its horn of tough, hard hair, has one of the strangest snouts.

# Glossary

**elephant seal** (EL-uh-fuhnt SEEL): a large sea mammal with four flippers; the male has a long, baggy snout

**mammals** (MAM-uhls): warm-blooded animals with fur that drink their mothers' milk

**predators** (PRED-uh-turs): animals that hunt other animals for food

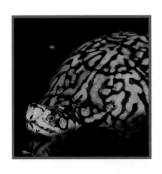

**scutes** (SKOOTS): hard scales that help protect reptitle shells and flesh

**snouts** (SNOUTS): the noses and most forward part on animals' faces

**spines** (SPINES): pointy growths found on some animals; often used for protection

# Index

dolphins    10, 11
elephant seal   8
porcupine    14, 15
predators    10
prey    10

sharks    10
snakes    18
spur    16, 17
turtles    18, 19

## Further Reading

Franks, Katie. *Turtles Up Close*. Powerkids Press, 2008.

Siedensticker, John. *Dangerous Animals*. Barnes and Noble, 2003.

Suen, Anastasia. *A Rhinoceros Grows Up*. Coughlan Publishing, 2005.

## Websites

www.zoofriends.org.au/childrens_activities/articles/spiky_animals.html
http://teacherportfolio.indstate.edu/hermit_firstgrade/spines.htm
www.pbs.org/wnet/nature/elephants/trunk.html

## About the Author

Lynn M. Stone is a widely-published wildlife and domestic animal photographer and the author of more than 500 children's books. His book *Box Turtles* was chosen as an Outstanding Science Trade Book and Selectors' Choice for 2008 by the Science Committee of the National Science Teachers' Association and the Children's Book Council.